I Like to Visit/Me gusta visitar

The Aquarium/ El acuario

Jacqueline Laks Gorman

Reading consultant/Consultora de lectura:
Susan Nations, M. Ed.,
author, literacy coach, consultant/
autora, tutora de alfabetización, consultora

WEEKLY READER

EARLY LEARNING LIBRARY

Please visit our web site at: www.garethstevens.com
For a free color catalog describing Weekly Reader® Early Learning Library's list
of high-quality books, call 1-877-445-5824 (USA) or 1-800-387-3178 (Canada).
Weekly Reader® Early Learning Library's fax: (414) 336-0164.

Library of Congress Cataloging-in-Publication Data available upon request from publisher.
Fax (414) 336-0157 for the attention of the Publishing Records Department.

ISBN 0-8368-4595-1 (lib. bdg.)
ISBN 0-8368-4602-8 (softcover)

This edition first published in 2005 by
Weekly Reader® Early Learning Library
A Member of the WRC Media Family of Companies
330 West Olive Street, Suite 100
Milwaukee, WI 53212 USA

Copyright © 2005 by Weekly Reader® Early Learning Library

Art direction: Tammy West
Editor: JoAnn Early Macken
Cover design and page layout: Kami Strunsee
Picture research: Diane Laska-Swanke
Translators: Tatiana Acosta and Guillermo Gutiérrez

Picture credits: Cover, pp. 5, 9, 13, 15, 17, 19, 21 Gregg Andersen; p. 7 © Gibson Stock
Photography; p. 11 © Kevin Schafer/SeaPics.com

All rights reserved. No part of this book may be reproduced, stored in a retrieval system,
or transmitted in any form or by any means, electronic, mechanical, photocopying,
recording, or otherwise, without the prior written permission of the copyright holder.

Printed in the United States of America

3 4 5 6 7 8 9 10 10 09 08 07 06

Note to Educators and Parents

Reading is such an exciting adventure for young children! They are beginning to integrate their oral language skills with written language. To encourage children along the path to early literacy, books must be colorful, engaging, and interesting; they should invite the young reader to explore both the print and the pictures.

I Like to Visit is a new series designed to help children read about familiar and exciting places. Each book explores a different place that kids like to visit and describes what a visitor can see and do there.

Each book is specially designed to support the young reader in the reading process. The familiar topics are appealing to young children and invite them to read — and re-read — again and again. The full-color photographs and enhanced text further support the student during the reading process.

In addition to serving as wonderful picture books in schools, libraries, homes, and other places where children learn to love reading, these books are specifically intended to be read within an instructional guided reading group. This small group setting allows beginning readers to work with a fluent adult model as they make meaning from the text. After children develop fluency with the text and content, the book can be read independently. Children and adults alike will find these books supportive, engaging, and fun!

— **Susan Nations, M.Ed., author/literacy coach/reading consultant**

Nota para los educadores y los padres

¡Leer es una aventura tan emocionante para los niños pequeños! A esta edad están comenzando a integrar su manejo del lenguaje oral con el lenguaje escrito. Para animar a los niños en el camino de la lectura incipiente, los libros deben ser coloridos, estimulantes e interesantes; deben invitar a los jóvenes lectores a explorar la letra impresa y las ilustraciones.

Me gusta visitar es una nueva colección diseñada para que los niños lean textos sobre lugares familiares y emocionantes. Cada libro explora un lugar diferente que a los niños les gustaría visitar, y describe lo que se puede ver y hacer en cada sitio.

Cada libro está especialmente diseñado para ayudar a los jóvenes lectores en el proceso de lectura. Los temas familiares llaman la atención de los niños y los invitan a leer —y releer— una y otra vez. Las fotografías a todo color y el tamaño de la letra ayudan aún más al estudiante en el proceso de lectura.

Además de servir como maravillosos libros ilustrados en escuelas, bibliotecas, hogares y otros lugares donde los niños aprenden a amar la lectura, estos libros han sido especialmente concebidos para ser leídos en un grupo de lectura guiada. Este contexto permite que los lectores incipientes trabajen con un adulto que domina la lectura mientras van determinando el significado del texto. Una vez que los niños dominan el texto y el contenido, el libro puede ser leído de manera independiente. ¡Estos libros les resultarán útiles, estimulantes y divertidos a niños y a adultos por igual!

— **Susan Nations, M.Ed., autora/tutora de alfabetización/consultora de desarrollo de la lectura**

I like to visit the aquarium. I can see ocean animals at the aquarium.

— — — — — — —

Me gusta visitar el acuario. En el acuario puedo ver animales del océano.

I can see fish at the aquarium. They swim behind big glass walls. They swim in a group called a **school**.

— — — — — — — —

En el acuario puedo ver peces. Los peces nadan detrás de grandes paredes de vidrio. Nadan en un grupo llamado **cardumen**.

I can see sharks at the aquarium.
Sharks have sharp teeth. Sharks
swim fast!

— — — — — — —

En el acuario puedo ver tiburones.
Los tiburones tienen dientes muy
afilados. ¡Y nadan muy rápido!

Knock, Knock...
Who's There?

I can see beluga whales at the aquarium. Beluga whales are white.

- - - - - - -

En el acuario puedo ver ballenas beluga. Las ballenas beluga son blancas.

I can see corals at the aquarium. The corals form a **reef**. Small, bright fish swim and hide in the reef.

━ ━ ━ ━ ━ ━ ━

En el acuario puedo ver corales. Los corales forman un **arrecife**. Pequeños peces de vivos colores nadan y se esconden en el arrecife.

CORAL Unlike fish and coral is a living animal, closely related to sea anemones and jellyfish. Each coral has a mouth and sting cells for catching plankton. Many corals build stony skeletons that create coral reefs. Most coral live in shallow water less than 200 feet from the surface and can be found near the Equator. However, some coral reefs can be found as deep as 1 League (18,228 feet), not 20,000 Leagues Under the Sea.

I can see sea horses, too. The male sea horse has a pouch. It is like a kangaroo's pocket. The sea horse carries its babies there.

▬ ▬ ▬ ▬ ▬ ▬ ▬

También puedo ver caballitos de mar. El macho tiene una bolsa, parecida a la de los canguros, donde lleva a sus crías.

I can touch some animals at the aquarium. I can touch a sea star. It feels bumpy.

- - - - - - -

En el acuario puedo tocar algunos animales. Puedo tocar una estrella de mar. Tiene muchos bultitos.

I like to watch the octopus. An octopus can change its colors.

■ ■ ■ ■ ■ ■ ■

Me gusta ver a los pulpos. Un pulpo puede cambiar de color.

I like to watch the dolphins, too.
The dolphins put on a show. They
leap! They dive! They splash!

— — — — — — — —

También me gusta ver a los
delfines. Los delfines montan
todo un espectáculo. ¡Saltan,
se sumergen y salpican mucha
agua!

21

Glossary

aquarium — a place where people can see water animals and plants

corals — tiny sea animals that live in groups and stay in one place. Corals leave hard skeletons when they die.

dolphins — air-breathing mammals that live in water. Dolphins look and act like fish.

reef — a ridge in the ocean made of corals, sand, or rocks

Glosario

acuario — lugar donde las personas pueden ver animales y plantas marinos

arrecife — barrera en el océano hecha de corales, arena o rocas

corales — animales marinos muy pequeños que viven en grupos y permanecen en un solo lugar. Cuando mueren, los corales dejan esqueletos duros.

delfines — mamíferos que respiran aire y viven en el agua. El aspecto y el comportamiento de los delfines es similar al de los peces.

For More Information/Más información

Books

Let's Go to the Aquarium. Weekend Fun (series). Cate Foley (Children's Press)
My Visit to the Aquarium. Aliki (HarperCollins)

Libros

El Caballito De Mar. Animales Acorazados. Lola Schaefer (Heinemann)
Nadarin. Leo Lionni (Plaza & Janes Editores, S.A.)

Web Sites

National Aquarium in Baltimore
www.aqua.org/animals.html
Photographs and information about fish

Páginas Web

Animales Acuario
www.zoomadrid.com/animales/archive/3/
Animales del acuario del zoológico de Madrid

Index

Índice

About the Author

Jacqueline Laks Gorman is a writer and editor. She grew up in New York City and began her career working on encyclopedias and other reference books. Since then, she has worked on many different kinds of books and written several children's books. She lives with her husband, David, and children, Colin and Caitlin, in DeKalb, Illinois. They all like to visit many kinds of places.

Información sobre la autora

Jacqueline Laks Gorman trabaja como escritora y editora. Jacqueline creció en la ciudad de Nueva York y comenzó su carrera trabajando en enciclopedias y otros libros de referencia. Desde entonces, ha trabajado en distintos tipos de libros y ha escrito varios libros para niños. Jacqueline vive con su esposo, David, y sus hijos, Colin y Caitlin, en DeKalb, Illinois. A toda la familia le gusta visitar distintos lugares.